Meet the SENATE

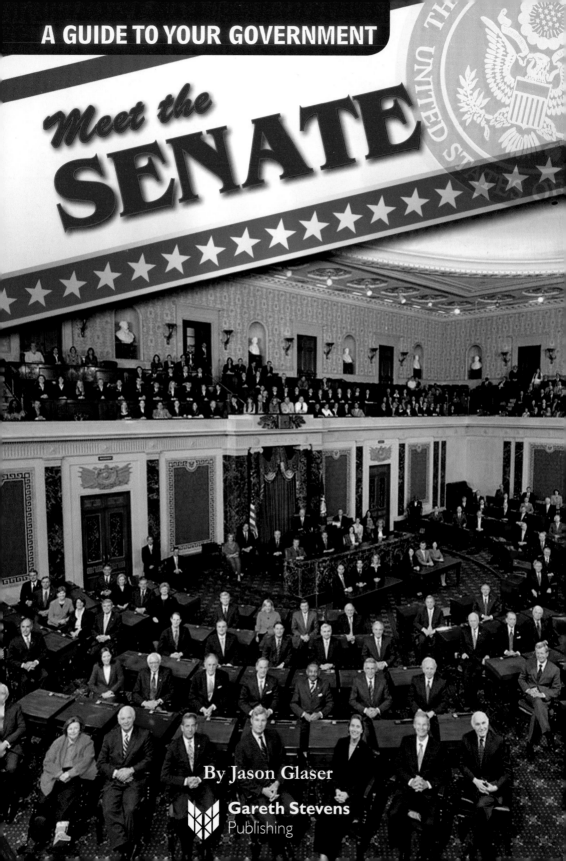

By Jason Glaser

Gareth Stevens
Publishing

Please visit our website, www.garethstevens.com. For a free color catalog of all our high-quality books, call toll free 1-800-542-2595 or fax 1-877-542-2596.

Library of Congress Cataloging-in-Publication Data

Glaser, Jason.
Meet the Senate / Jason Glaser.
    p. cm. — (A guide to your government)
Includes index.
ISBN 978-1-4339-7264-5 (pbk.)
ISBN 978-1-4339-7265-2 (6-pack)
ISBN 978-1-4339-7267-6 (library binding)
1. United States. Congress. Senate—Juvenile literature. I. Title.
JK1276.G53 2012
328.73'071—dc23

                              2012005938

First Edition

Published in 2013 by
Gareth Stevens Publishing
111 East 14th Street, Suite 349
New York, NY 10003

Designer: Daniel Hosek
Editor: Kristen Rajczak

Photo credits: Cover, p. 1 U.S. Senate, 111th Congress, Senate Photo Studio; p. 5 (main image) Saul Loeb/AFP/Getty Images; p. 5 (Roman Senate) Universal History Archive/Getty Images; pp. 6–7 MPI/Getty Images; p. 9 Robyn Beck/AFP/Getty Images; p. 11 Eric Thayer/Getty Images; p. 13 Tim Sloan/AFP/Getty Images; p. 15 (main image) Chuck Kennedy/MCT/Getty Images; p. 15 (McCarthy) AFP/Getty Images; p. 17 Hank Walker/Time & Life Pictures/Getty Images; p. 19 (main) Library of Congress/Getty Images; p. 19 (Johnson) Stock Montage/Getty Images; p. 21 Omikron Omikron/Getty Images; p. 23 Marshall/Getty Images; p. 25 Emmanuel Dunand/AFP/Getty Images; p. 27 Mark Wilson/Getty Images; p. 29 Win McNamee/Getty Images.

Printed in the United States of America

CPSIA compliance information: Batch #CS12GS: For further information contact Gareth Stevens, New York, New York at 1-800-542-2595.

CONTENTS

Words in the glossary appear in **bold** type
the first time they are used in the text.

A SELECT FEW

On January 5, 2011, the 112th Congress met for its first session to continue the work begun at the birth of the US **Constitution** in 1789. The 100 members of the Senate, two from each state, included 83 men and 17 women.

Greater in number than the 22 senators who first met in New York City more than 200 years ago, the senators working in our capital today carry tremendous power. The US Senate and the House of Representatives make up the legislative, or lawmaking, branch of the US government. Together, they are called Congress. As one-half of Congress, the Senate has a large impact on the laws of our nation. Its duties greatly affect the other branches of government as well.

FEDERAL *Fact*

The first time the Senate met was on March 4, 1789. However, there weren't enough senators present to legally hold the session. It was April before more arrived and the group could begin working.

The Roman Senate

The US Senate is modeled in part after a similar system used in ancient Rome. The word "senate" comes from the Latin word *senex*, meaning "old man." At first, Roman senators came from the wealthiest and most powerful families in Rome. Later, common people also sat on the senate, though some of them weren't allowed to speak! Roman senators' terms were for life.

Each new Senate session begins in January of odd-numbered years, after elections are held the previous November.

THE GREAT COMPROMISE

The first national government of the independent American colonies was formed under the Articles of Confederation. After going into effect in 1781, the Articles established a government with a weak legislative branch made up of a one-house Congress. Each state had only one vote, but the number of delegates ranged from two to seven.

In 1787, state representatives met to strengthen the Articles. At this meeting, which became known as the Constitutional Convention,

FEDERAL *Fact*

At the convention, another compromise was made with slave-holding southern states. They were allowed to count each slave as three-fifths of a person toward their population, increasing their representation in Congress.

the US Constitution was written. During the convention, big and small states struck a deal. The new legislative branch would be made up of two bodies—the House of Representatives and the Senate. States would each have two senators and a number of representatives based on population. Both houses would have to agree on laws before they could pass.

Upper and Lower

The US Senate is sometimes called the "Upper House." Since there are fewer senators, each vote in the Senate has a greater impact. Many senators have come to feel that this makes them more important than House representatives, which led to the House of Representatives being nicknamed the "Lower House." However, the House and Senate are each important to the legislative process.

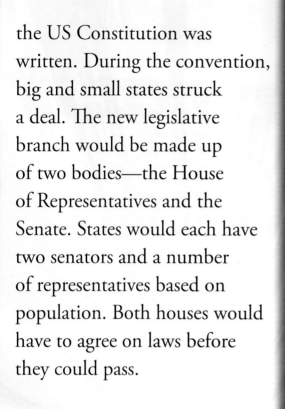

This painting shows convention delegates signing the US Constitution.

BY THE PEOPLE

At first it was up to each state's legislature to choose the senators who would represent the state. The authors of the Constitution felt this would create a bond between the federal government and state governments. This process had flaws. State legislatures were often slow to name new senators or couldn't agree on a candidate. This left the Senate with too many open seats, and it was hard to get work done.

By 1900, several states were already moving toward direct election of senators. People feared that senators were more interested in pleasing state legislators than citizens. In 1912, Congress proposed an amendment to change the election process. The following year, most states **ratified** the Seventeenth Amendment, which stated that US Senators would now be chosen by **popular vote**.

FEDERAL *Fact*

The Seventeenth Amendment also gives state governors the ability to name someone to fill a seat left empty by a senator who quit or died. This person remains in office until a special election can be held.

By moving to popular voting for its members, the Senate could avoid unfair or illegal choices by the state legislatures.

Keeping Good Company

The Constitution states that the US Senate has the right to accept or refuse a senator after a contested election. This could include an election in which the votes are being counted again, or if the candidate is suspected of breaking election laws. The Senate has done this many times. In 1926, the Senate believed Illinois's chosen senator, Frank Smith, hadn't been elected fairly. He was refused his Senate seat for more than 2 years before he finally resigned.

GETTING A SEAT

Senators are elected for 6-year terms. Once in office, a senator can run for reelection as many times as he or she chooses. The Constitution sets forth three qualifications for senate candidates. Senators must be 30 years old, must have been a US citizen for at least 9 years, and must be a resident of the state in which they are elected.

Nearly all senators belong to a political party. In the Senate chamber, senators who are Democrats usually sit on the left side, and Republican senators sit on the right. When senators caucus, or meet together outside the chamber, they often separate by party. Each party's senators discuss their plans and how they will vote in upcoming sessions.

FEDERAL *Fact*

As of 2012, Robert Byrd of West Virginia had served longer than any other senator. He served over half a century—from January 3, 1959, to June 28, 2010.

Slow to Act Can Be Good

The US Senate is made for long, thoughtful work. The Founding Fathers hoped the longer terms would make the Senate think about the future—not just popular opinion. The terms of the senators are organized so that only one-third are up for reelection at a time. Also, two senators from the same state aren't scheduled to run for reelection in the same year. These rules free senators to act carefully and make good decisions.

Special elections, or those occurring outside the normal election cycle, may cause two senators from the same state to be elected in the same year. In 1992, California voters elected both Barbara Boxer and Dianne Feinstein to the Senate.

Barbara Boxer

Dianne Feinstein

BEHIND THE SCENES

All senators serve on a number of committees and subcommittees. These groups focus on a particular area of government, such as foreign relations, agriculture, or finance. Since thousands of bills are **sponsored** each session, committee members must pick the bills they think the Senate should discuss. Only those bills have a chance to become laws.

Committees have a chair, or leader, who guides the group. The chair is chosen from the majority political party and is usually the senator with the most seniority in that committee. Chairs have great power in deciding which bills to work on. The consideration of a bill can be a long process, which involves "marking up," or changing a bill's wording or requirements. Committees and subcommittees also hold hearings when working on a bill.

FEDERAL Fact

Some committees meet with representatives from the House of Representatives who are working on the same issues. These meetings are called joint committees.

Senate committees try to craft bills that have the best chance to pass on the Senate floor.

Seniority

The length of time a senator is in office is a key factor in picking chairs and committees. Those who have more time in office, or seniority, are given special treatment when committee assignments are made. The tradition of recognizing seniority began during the 1840s. Today, being a more senior senator yields other benefits, too. For example, they are allowed to choose desks closer to the front of the chamber!

As committees and subcommittees think about bills and laws, they usually speak with outside experts. These are people with experience and knowledge that may be helpful in deciding if certain laws would be effective.

Most of the time, experts are happy to give their opinion to the Senate. If the Senate is investigating shameful or illegal behavior, however, witnesses may not want to **testify** or provide information. In these cases, the Senate can **subpoena** them to turn over needed papers or force them to come to Washington, DC, to meet.

After hearings and markup sessions, committees must decide if a bill is ready to become a law. If they think it is, the bill is turned over to the full Senate for discussion and a possible vote.

★ ★ ★ ★ ★ ★ ★ ★ ★ ★ ★ ★ ★ ★ ★ ★ ★ ★ ★

FEDERAL Fact

Some committees and subcommittees are standing, or permanent, while others are temporary and created when needed.

★ ★ ★ ★ ★ ★ ★ ★ ★ ★ ★ ★ ★ ★ ★ ★ ★ ★ ★

Joseph McCarthy

Joseph McCarthy

During 1953 and 1954, there was one committee very few people wanted to speak with: the Senate Permanent Subcommittee on Investigations. Its chairman, Senator Joseph McCarthy from Wisconsin, used the subcommittee to search for **Communists** in the federal government, national organizations, and even the US Army. He demanded information from hundreds of people. McCarthy was so forceful that the Senate later changed the rules of hearings to give witnesses more protection.

In 2008, baseball star Roger Clemens testified in front of a Senate committee investigating the use of drugs in baseball. Two years later, he was charged with perjury because the committee believed he lied.

Roger Clemens

SPEAKING FREELY

Although politics can turn senators into bitter enemies, they must treat each other with respect while **debating** in session. Senators often refer to each other as "the honorable Senator from" followed by the name of the senator's home state.

There aren't many rules about the length of debates in the Senate. Senators can speak as long as needed about an issue. However, sometimes senators try to block a vote on a bill by talking endlessly. This process is called "filibustering." The use of the filibuster caused the Senate to adopt a cloture rule, which forces a senator to end a speech. Today, it takes three-fifths of all senators to vote for cloture. The threat of filibuster may cause the bill's supporters to accept changes to it they might not otherwise consider.

FEDERAL Fact

Insulting a fellow senator can result in censure, or a call to publicly shame a person for wrongdoing by the other members of a group.

Long-Winded Senators

The longest Senate filibuster came from Senator Strom Thurmond of South Carolina in 1957. He spoke and answered questions for 24 hours and 18 minutes straight in order to block a bill. The tactic was tried again in 1964, when many senators combined their filibusters into a 57-day delay before cloture, which then required a two-thirds vote, was reached. Both of these filibusters came from Southern senators trying to block civil rights laws.

Senator Olin Johnston is pictured here with the 750-page filibuster speech he wrote in 1957 to try and stop a bill about voting rights.

CHECKS AND BALANCES

Governmental powers are divided so that no one person or group has too much power. This system is called checks and balances. A bill might pass in the Senate, but a matching bill still must pass in the House. Even then, the president, the head of the executive branch of the United States, might **veto** the bill. If he does, the House and the Senate can override the veto with a two-thirds vote and make the bill a law anyway.

The Senate even has some control over the judicial branch of government. This is made up of federal courts and the highest court, the US Supreme Court. The president names candidates to the Supreme Court, but the Senate must approve them. The Senate must approve other high-ranking presidential **appointments** as well.

FEDERAL Fact

A bill can begin in either the House or the Senate, except those dealing with money. Bills regarding money or taxation all start in the House.

After Andrew Johnson became the first president to be impeached, the Senate was one vote short of removing him from office in 1868.

Andrew Johnson

Impeachment

Another check the legislative branch has is the ability to impeach officials in all branches of government, including judges and even the president! Impeachment means an official is investigated for illegal activities while still in office. Only the House can impeach, but the Senate holds the trial. If the Senate finds the person guilty, that person is removed from office. Presidents Andrew Johnson and William Clinton were impeached, but both avoided removal.

19

AGREEMENTS BETWEEN NATIONS

The Constitution states that the Senate and the president share power in making treaties. A treaty can be as big as promising not to wage war or as small as cooperating in sending mail between countries. The Senate's main job is to advise the president about the treaties and then approve or reject them.

After the president or a presidential representative works with another country or countries to write a treaty, it's submitted to the Senate for discussion. The Senate may approve the treaty as is or ask that changes be made. Sometimes, a treaty will spend years in committee! If the treaty passes the Senate with a two-thirds vote, the president can formally accept its terms.

FEDERAL *Fact*
Between 1939 and 1989, the United States approved an average of 250 treaties each year.

The Treaty of Versailles

A peace treaty called the Treaty of Versailles ended World War I and established the League of Nations, an organization of governments that would work to peacefully solve problems between countries. US president Woodrow Wilson strongly supported the treaty and the league. However, the Senate wanted changes to be made to the treaty. Wilson was against these changes, and the Senate rejected the treaty. As a result, the United States didn't join the league. The Senate's rejection greatly embarrassed President Wilson.

Though Congress didn't approve the Treaty of Versailles, the signing of which is shown here, it did pass a list of resolutions in 1921 formally ending the United States' conflict with Germany and Austria-Hungary.

LEADERSHIP IN THE SENATE

The Constitution names the vice president of the United States as the president of the Senate. However, the only power the vice president has is to cast a vote in the event of a tie in the Senate. He also presides over, or leads, the Senate, though his schedule doesn't often allow time for this. When the vice president isn't present, the president pro tempore presides. The longest-serving member of the majority party is usually elected to this position.

The Senate has created other leadership roles over time. The Senate majority and minority parties each elect a leader to be their main spokesperson. Each party also uses secondary leaders called whips. Whips are responsible for finding out how each party member plans to vote and making sure they attend important votes.

FEDERAL Fact

The president pro tempore doesn't run the entire Senate session, but usually asks new senators to lead at times. This helps new, or freshman, senators learn the Senate rules.

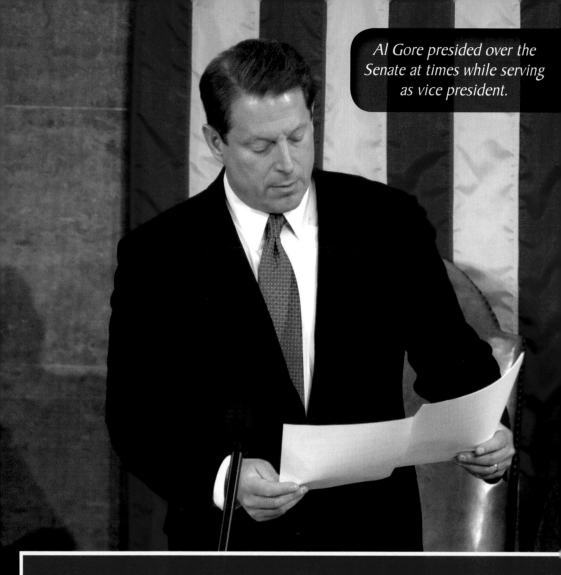

Al Gore presided over the Senate at times while serving as vice president.

Tradition and the Senate

The Constitution gives the Senate the freedom to set its own rules. These rules are designed to make debates orderly and effective. Some rules are standing rules, such as how the Senate session begins every day. There are also rules that come from Senate tradition. One tradition has the leaders of the political parties sit in the front seats on each side of the center aisle. Many other traditions date back to the first Senate session.

23

The Senate and House are equal politically, but having a 6-year term and a vote equaling 1 percent of the Senate carries a lot of political power. Many senators have used their positions as a path to even higher office. As of 2012, 16 presidents had first served as senators.

Barack Obama is a prime example of this rise to the presidency. From being elected to the Illinois State Senate in 1996, Obama moved on to be elected to the US Senate in 2004. He represented Illinois in the Senate for only 3 years before announcing he would run for president. Some people didn't think this was enough time to gain the necessary experience to be president. Nonetheless, Obama won the election in 2008.

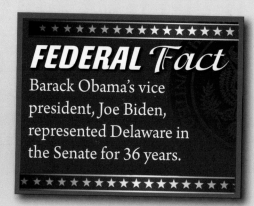

FEDERAL Fact

Barack Obama's vice president, Joe Biden, represented Delaware in the Senate for 36 years.

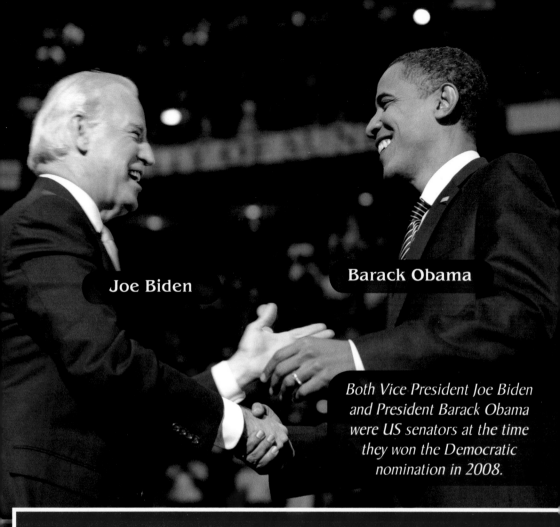

Joe Biden

Barack Obama

Both Vice President Joe Biden and President Barack Obama were US senators at the time they won the Democratic nomination in 2008.

Costly Campaigns

In addition to the requirements the Constitution sets for being a senator, other circumstances may limit who can run for Senate. Candidates often need to spend a lot of money to get elected. Some candidates have to drop out of races because they run out of money. In 2008, the average amount spent by the winning senators was $8.5 million. Candidates often use their own money to run, but most have to raise money from supporters, too.

NOTABLE SENATORS

Senator Daniel Inouye of Hawaii has served in the Senate since 1963. By serving his full term to 2014, he will become the longest-serving senator in history.

Senators Bernie Sanders of Vermont and Joe Liebermann of Connecticut hold unique positions in the Senate. Although they caucus with the Democrats, Liebermann and Sanders are Independents, or part of neither major party. Both parties have regularly sought their support during tight votes.

A growing number of women serve in the Senate. Maine is notable for having had women as both its senators from the 1990s to 2012: Olympia Snowe and Susan Collins. Their service is remarkable considering that, as of 2011, only 39 women have ever been senators.

FEDERAL *Fact*

The first woman senator was an honorary appointment from Georgia. Senator Rebecca Latimer Felton served for only 1 day: November 21, 1922.

Diversity in the Senate

The US Senate has been slow in coming to resemble the growing **diversity** of the United States. Besides the 39 women, the US Senate has only had 3 Native American senators, 6 African Americans, and 7 Hispanic Americans. There have also been 6 Asian Americans, 5 hailing from Hawaii's sizable Asian American population.

THE FUTURE OF THE SENATE

One interesting possibility about the US Senate's future would be if another state joined the United States. Should a **territory** like Puerto Rico be approved for statehood, two more senators would join the Upper House. This would change the number of senators needed for a majority.

Another major change would be if even more **third-party** candidates were elected. A number of different political parties have come and gone throughout our nation's history. The rise of more third-party senators would make it harder for Republicans or Democrats to have a majority. Bills would probably require additional compromise in order to pass.

However the Senate changes in coming years, it will certainly continue to fulfill its duties and work toward a better future for our nation.

FEDERAL *Fact*

Other political parties that have held a majority in the Senate include the Federalists and the Whigs.

In the 2010 Congressional election, many candidates ran as Tea Party members.

Rand Paul

The Senate and the Internet

Today, US citizens have more access to the political process than ever before. Senate proceedings are regularly streamed on the Internet. Government websites keep people up to date on the most recent events. E-mail allows people to communicate directly and instantly with their senator or the senator's office. People interested in Senate politics can study the process without having to travel to Washington, DC. Those wishing to run for office can even use the Internet to gather support!

GLOSSARY

appointment: an official position filled by a person selected by the president

Communist: a member of the Communist party, which believed in shared ownership of property and goods

Constitution: the piece of writing that states the laws of the United States

debate: to discuss an issue by presenting all sides. Also, the discussion itself.

diversity: the condition of including different groups

popular vote: the combined individual votes of all citizens who cast a vote

ratify: to give legal approval

sponsor: to take ownership of a bill and be the leading voice in trying to get the bill passed

subpoena: a document that orders a person to either appear in court or face being arrested

territory: a part of the United States that isn't within any state and has its own legislature

testify: to make a formal statement of truth

third-party: having to do with an organized political group with leaders who aren't members of the two leading political parties

veto: the power to stop something from becoming law. Also, to reject.

FOR MORE INFORMATION

★★★★★★★★★★★★★★★★★★★★★★★

Books

Dubois, Muriel L. *The U.S. Senate*. Mankato, MN: Capstone Press, 2004.

Jakubiak, David J. *What Does a Senator Do?* New York, NY: PowerKids Press, 2010.

Jones, Veda Boyd. *The Senate*. Philadelphia, PA: Chelsea House, 2000.

Websites

Congress for Kids: Legislative Branch – the Senate
congressforkids.net/Legislativebranch_senate.htm
Learn historical facts about the Senate, find out who your senator is, and further understand how the Senate works.

The United States Senate
www.senate.gov
The official page for the Senate includes history, resources for reference, tools for interacting with the government, and information about current events and legislation.

INDEX